Heal Yourself!

The New Way of Healing Yourself and
Overcoming Emotional Trouble: How to
Focus on Your Inner Voice, Start Loving
Yourself and Unleash Your Mind from
Negative Thoughts

Amber M. Gardner

Table of Contents

The Importance Of 'You'

You. A short word, and yet the most important thing in the world. One syllable. Three letters. Why. Oh. You.

So simple, and yet it comprises everything you know, remember and care about. Every electrical impulse that makes up the fiber of your being, every fact you have ever heard and retained, every emotion ever felt or displayed. Everything that manifests in the totality of your existence. A simple, short, snappy word, used every day as one of the seven thousand words in the average daily vocabulary, amongst less meaningful words of the same length, and yet it probably comprises the most complexity out of any word in the English language. Words like transubstantiation or circumnavigation are longer, and seem more complex, but really, *you* is a much more complicated word, due to a highly complex myriad of meanings, which one can never fully understand.

Why is this a big deal, you might ask yourself? And why have I spent an entire paragraph delineating its importance? Well, I'll tell you.

Because *you are the most important thing in the world.*

Sounds crazy?

Egotistical?

Self obsessed?

Any number of negative traits come to mind when you read that sentence, no? Well, put it this way. Everything you know is You. Everything you've ever seen is You. Everything that you understand about politics, world events, and the fabric of the universe, is You.

So really, without a You, these things can not be at all.

There's an argument to be made that these things simply *are*, and always *have been*, before you were born, and indeed, long after you are dead, but consider this -

without a You, these things may as well not exist. At all. Because without You, they aren't. I mean, of course, they *are*, but without your consciousness, they simply *aren't*, because *you* are not there to experience them, and by extension, they are not. I promise this will be the last time I get Aristotelian on you.

Now, take this fact - and it is, reader, a *fact* - and consider that when talking about things like politics, world events, and the fabric of the Universe, we are referring to outward things. External things. We learn about each of them as we go through life. We are taught about them when we go, self conscious and anxiety riddled, through school. They are drilled into us as we bend ourselves into the shape of a mould that we don't necessarily fit into; we are play doh who are shaped both to whatever substance society deems acceptable, and also to what is cool, due to how our social development implores us through its pressure. We are bombarded by these things as we take our exams and go to college, and then when we start our working lives, the play doh that makes up our being has begun to solidify.

Of course, by this point it is our *choice* whether or not to learn about these things, but I digress.

We switch on the TV (or hell, although terrestrial telly is surely something we can *circumnavigate* nowadays with all of the streaming and self appointed entertainment options that we have at our disposal today, but if you go on Twitter you'll see Tweets from the Mars Perseverance Rover, so even then there is no escape from this pesky, external fabric of the universe stuff, but I digress again) and there's the news. World events. Politics. Societal things. The Universe. Of course, at this point in our lives, these things might all simply be options to us, things we don't necessarily have to take an interest in, and yet, nevertheless they are unequivocally there. Things we can't avoid. They seep into our lives in one way or another. External realities. Things that are simply out of our control, but that nonetheless affect our daily lives, no matter the depth of our interest in them.

The point I am making here is that throughout our lives, we are bombarded by external things that we have little control over, while the internal strife builds and builds.

Self doubt, anxiety, existential questioning, depression, grief, loss, frustration, questions of *what's the point* and *why was I born* and even times of self deprecation, pervade our subconscious and infest our inner voice with negative possibilities, and your teachers, who taught you algebra, basic English skills, and standard science, never told you how to process this stuff, or how to deal with it.

At no point during your school days were you ever taught how deal with failing your driving test, or achieving underwhelming results in an important exam, or what to do when you have a big deadline coming up and there's just *not enough time*, or how to go on in the seconds, hours and days after your partner dumps you, or how to cope with working full time while feeling at any moment you could break down and cry as a result of any number of circumstances. Nobody gave you one inkling of an idea how to deal with life, and to a greater extent, how to cope with *yourself*. It's a tough one, and often something we have to teach ourselves, because it is all up to us. Some of us, in fact, do. It's hard, and it takes a long time, and a great deal of inner searching, and needless to say, even a great deal of suffering. Much suffering. I'd say inhumane suffering, but let's face it, we all face these hardships, and they certainly are not inhumane, because they are universal, and so they are by very definition, *humane*. It's a tough fact of life to accept that these things are simply what it means to be human. Nobody taught us how difficult they would be, and nobody gave us a mental tool to deal with them. Things go wrong in life. Sometimes we are unable to help others, and the fact of the matter is, these things occur as a result of *cognitive dissonance brought on by a negative inner voice.*

Yes, you can psychoanalyse each and every one of the things listed here, and come up with reams and reams and reams of information of why such things exist, and the answers that great philosophers have discussed at length, but ultimately it all comes down to you and how you perceive things. The voices in our heads are loud.

Much louder than the facts we retain, and so, if we can change the perceptions of our encounters, and the way that we process them, then we can change the way our inner voice speaks to us. This, in turn, will increase productivity, acceptance, and give us a manageable skill base through which to deal with internal strife, and that is an impressive and useful set of tools. A complicated set, but sure enough, one that will help you out time and time again day to day.

You are the most important thing in the Universe. You are the carbon that makes up all life. Now, act like it.

Your Inner Voice

Let's go right for the jugular and discuss the inner voice.

It is absolutely true that the inner voice is a complicated thing. It can materialise as your best friend, equally take the form of your worst enemy, and it can even be both of those things at the same time. It can be an overwhelmingly bright dazzle of light, that sets off electricity in your blood, or it can be black bile trudging around your veins. But more often than not, it is somewhere in between the two.

Whatever state it may exist in, the inner voice is relatively simple by its definition. It is the sum total of your brain chemistry and thought habits. After all, aren't we all just electrical organisms responding to constant data? Chemical reactions occur perpetually, creating new and interesting emotions and states.

There are certain basics that are universal, which when applied correctly, will provide our brain chemistry with a certain amount of ballast. Water, exercise and a good source of nutrients, to be exact, and these we will discuss later in some more depth, but for now, let's just accept that these are things that we can control. When our brain chemistry is well balanced, and our bodies have received everything that they need, we can find a degree of health in our inner workings. The body is a circuit, after all. An engine. And it needs fuel to survive, and should be treated as such to a certain degree.

But not quite.

As human beings, we are much more complicated than an engine. The most well adjusted of us may be just fine and dandy with a job, three good meals a day, and occasional sex, but those of us with louder inner voices often need more than that. Does your inner voice sometimes sound a little something like this?

You are no good. Everything you have ever done has been attained falsely, and everybody who loves you does so under false pretenses. They don't know the real you. They tolerate you, they don't really love you. And what the hell did you say that for? He thinks you're a complete twat now. And look, now you've overcooked your food. Can't even put a meal together. Wow. And look, just LOOK at the sum total of your day. You've done nothing, and consequently you are nothing.

There is a lot of pop psychology in there. To start with, an absolute sense of imposter syndrome, a spoonful of an inferiority complex, and some pretty intense anxiety, which, whenever invited to a party, consequently brings along her uninvited, big, buff, miserable brother - depression. But these are the kinds of thought spirals that are a reality for many. Many people today periodically feel this way, and it is an important thing to learn to navigate, if we are to learn to navigate it at all.

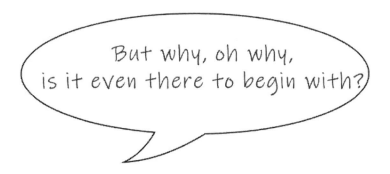

But why, oh why,
is it even there to begin with?

For some people these thoughts might materialise as a result of purely external forces - an argument with their partner, a scalding from their boss, a bad day in general, or all of the above - and indeed, these are valid, and are important to attend to. However, it can be equally difficult when these thought processes begin as a result of, well, nothing we can put our finger on. When we wake up and - BAM - badness.

But what's going on?
where did I go wrong?

I feel you. I really do.

It is also important to clarify that the 'badness' I am referring to is broad and can take many different forms. We all have our own demons that periodically come out to stick their claws in our porridge, and our individual needs are different.

So what can we do in these instances? In the descent of badness.

The temptation, and we're all guilty of our own version of this from time to time, is to retreat to our beds and stare at the ceiling until these thoughts start to fade away, and we are fortunate that for the most part, the bad things tend to fade away after a healthy amount of retreat time. Our brains only have so much time to worry about things, and so if a negative thought or emotion is spiralling around and around our minds, it is a fact that eventually it will exhaust itself, spread out like a gas and disappear. The trouble is, and can be, that often these things aren't simply *thoughts*, they are *emotions*. It's just that the emotions create the thoughts, and the thoughts enhance the emotions. If you want to nuke the problem at its prime source, you have to focus on the emotions themselves, the thought spirals that exacerbate these conditions, and there are a few different techniques we can enforce in order to deal with these.

Yes, as mentioned before, shutting yourself away and letting the emotion exhaust itself can be helpful, and you shouldn't beat yourself up if that is what you need. In fact, the school of thought that I derive from personally is the one that says that *it is okay* to quarantine yourself for your own good from time to time. Nobody can tell you how to deal with your own issues, and so go ahead. Do what you must.

But bear in mind the practices that can be introduced to alleviate these emotions, and use them when you are quarantined. Differently, if you are the sort to charge ahead and go through life anyhow, these practices can be employed at many times throughout the day, so don't think of this as a solitary activity. That is, in a nutshell, what these solutions I will now describe to you are. Practices.

Firstly, a bit of meditation can go a long way in a situation like this. Just close the door, breathe deeply, and look into the darkness and the silence. The simple act of breathing deeply through one's nose comes handy in this practice. It has an instant calming effect on the brain. Keep it up ten or twenty times, and just imagine all of the stress lifting off of you, up up up into the air, through the roof, and away, gone. Clear your head of all thoughts. It's just you on a cliff with the clouds and the sunset. There? Okay, let's go.

Consider the above voice and all its negative destruction. Is there anything that we can do to turn it around? Or, at the very least, alleviate it so that the pain is *absolutely minimal?* It might feel hopeless during an emotional time, or your brain might just be too stubborn at the time to accept the potential of a solution, and I can empathize with that to a humongous degree, but remember, some things *are* in our control. Sometimes a mindset categorically *is* a choice you can make. Consider that, and then take the first allegation.

You are no good.

Look at this. Examine it. Realise the falsehood in it. You are no good? Then how did you achieve every single thing you ever achieved? How did you land that job? How did you make that particular friend? Did you get up and wash the dishes today? *Good.* That *counts.*

When feeling these emotions, it is important to consider the things that you can reach out and touch. The fact that you were even able to get up and make your bed counts. Taking any step, in any particular direction, counts. If you are functioning and have achieved anything, and I mean *any small thing,* then this statement can not possibly be true, and we haven't even looked at anything substantial yet. I'm certain that you, reader, and any other reader, will be able to account for any one of the three possibilities listed above, and by extension, you will be able to account for so much more than that.

Everything you have ever done has been attained falsely.

Hello, imposter syndrome! Nice to see you again, old friend. Hey, guess what, you are absolutely full of shit!

Reader, nothing is attained falsely. Unless you are a thief, or somebody who hired an outsider to write your dissertation for you, or sent a surrogate version of yourself out to do your job interview for you, and your surrogate just happened to be a completely different human being to you entirely, then guess what? You have not attained a single thing in your life falsely.

There are a great many excuses we can make for our achievements in life. "Oh, that wasn't done right," or "I got that only because I had a friend who worked there...oh no, that doesn't count, that assignment was tailored to me, I didn't really achieve it..."

Nonsense. You did it. Nobody else. You.

You, reader, you.

When confronted by imposter syndrome, it is important to bear in mind what you achieved, what it means, and particularly, how a stranger might react to it. Has a new person ever listened to you talking about yourself and raised their eyebrows with incredulity and said, "You what? No, that's wrong. You scumbag."

I'll bet the answer is no. I'll bet they aren't even interested enough to think on that level, but the people who listen, will probably be fascinated by your achievements. I'll even bet that they might admire you, in some instances. Most of the time, they simply don't care, but that's life. So there is only one place for imposter syndrome. It must be invalidated by us. How do we do this? By recognising our achievements. Stick with this book and I'll show you a few ways that you can do that. But for now, let's move on through these false statements.

Everybody who loves you does so under false pretenses.

This is simply impossible. If you feel fake, look around you. Nobody is ever their entire undisputed selves. In fact, let's take this further. While I fundamentally believe in the concept of You, I feel completely different about that of the self. There is no self. Self is an illusion. There is no doubt that human beings are the imagination of themselves. However, the illusion of self can never be lost. The narcissism of identity as a concept can simply not be derailed, nor should it. But the fact is that a human being is a brain connected to a body, chemical reactions in the brain are constant and endless from the moment we are conceived until the moment we die. Emotions are electrical impulses that happen within our brain chemistry. There is no self, only a fluid, flowing set of chemistry that circulates us twenty four hours a day, every day.

But getting that rant out of the way, let's explore that a bit more when tackling the next false statement. Let's just suffice right now with: *There is no such thing as false pretense.*

They don't know the real you. They tolerate you, they don't really love you.

Again, there is no self, and so whatever you perceive the real you to be, just know that any aspect of yourself that you choose to reveal, any alley that your personality might stem from, is never false, even if your words are untrue. Words are only words. Human beings have been on this planet for around two hundred thousand years, and language has only been a thing for maybe two thirds of that time, at a push. So how then, if life is older than language, can we be said to be false on any level, when society evolved without language? When humans hunted, gathered, mated and continued without the lying gene's dominance?

Demeanour and mannerism is so much more than that.

But this is simply an inaccurate statement. There is a reason that the people in your life are in your life, and that is that.

And what the hell did you say that for? He thinks you're a complete twat now.

Classic anxiety. Here's the thing: Nobody cares about your words as much as you do. That's right. Nobody thinks as hard about these things. They're usually over in a flash. In a social gathering, after a conversation ends, other conversations pervade and cancel said conversations out, almost. Every tiny little meaning that can be deduced from one awkward conversation is not worth dwelling on. See that you can train yourself to not give these thought processes any more time than they are worth.

And look, now you've overcooked your food. Can't even put a meal together. Wow.

On bad days, something as small as a meal can seem like a big deal. It isn't. You have done many great things with your day, and your life, and nothing so simple as a meal or a spilt cup of tea, or anything of that nature, defines you in any way.

And look, just LOOK at the sum total of your day. You've done nothing, and consequently you are nothing.

This is very much the bottom line when it comes to these emotions. *You are nothing.* Your brain tells you that the very fibre of your being is useless, or incapable, or any number of things. In extreme cases, this can lead to darker thoughts.

I am nothing, everything is futile, I may as well kill myself.

It is easy to let one thing after another build and build until we are in distress. Emotions are more powerful than logic (emotions in fact, like language, are much older than logic). But, perhaps some insight into how it works will help put it in the most basic terms possible, and by extension, shed some light on why and how these emotions can become more intense with the increased focus on them.

The thing is, satisfying your emotions is the same as procrastination, in that entertaining them satisfies the limbic system, just like having a cookie or a beer on impulse. The limbic system is essentially a part of the brain buried very, very deep inside of the head, and is a very primitive part of the brain (hence the depth which it is buried in your head) It is much, much much *much* older than the prefrontal cortex, the part of the brain that does all of the long term planning, the logistical strategies, the deductive reasoning, and critical thinking. Bluntly put, it is the part of the brain responsible for your logical thinking. Thoughts such as, "I really ought to get some work done today, or else I am going to fall behind," come from the prefrontal cortex. But the limbic system operates on a different level, and its power is greater than that of the prefrontal cortex. Ergo, it is much easier to satisfy. So next time you are down in emotional despair, just try to remember that this is not a logical part of your brain, and ask yourself, can it truly be fully trusted as a reliable spirit level to test your anxieties and worries against?

But in the end, these emotions *exhaust themselves.* Nothing is permanent. Every feeling is temporary, and this is especially true in regards to many of the bad ones. So do yourself a favour and practice the art of paying them less heed. Again, I will discuss this further in later essays.

Now, is there another way that we can look at this thought spiral? Is there any way that we can work it around so that it is something more practical, and realistic?

This is a tough practice to enforce during our emotionally stressful periods, but it is the act of recontextualising our thoughts.

You are doing fine. Everything you have ever done was attained by you, and everybody who loves you does so because you are you. They love you for who you are, regardless of your faults. They are here for a reason. They really do love you. And sure, you might have said something that you consider makes you look silly, but there's no way that the other person is thinking on the same deep level about it as you. And sure, maybe the food was overcooked, but it doesn't matter because it's only lunch. Wow. And look, just LOOK at the sum total of your day. You might feel like you've done nothing, but look, the reality is that you achieved plenty, and anyway, it doesn't matter, because there is always tomorrow, always now.

There. Now, say it aloud. Let your ears hear it. Allow your brain (which is as malleable as anything and will accept pretty much anything that you throw at it if you throw it hard enough) to soak it in, to process it subconsciously. Now say it again. There.

This is a practice, and the more you do it, the more you can turn the untrustworthy sludge that's trudging through your brain into something that is much more realistic in terms of reality. Remember, this is your inner voice, and the path to improving it is one of recognition. That is, recognising the falsehoods in it and learning which emotions to practice discarding and which to use.

You are no good.
Everything you have ever done
has been attained falsely, and everybody
who loves you does so under false pretenses.
They don't know the real you. They tolerate you,
they don't really love you. And what the hell did you
say that for? He thinks you're a complete twat now.
And look, now you've overcooked your food. Can't even
put a meal together. Wow. And look, just LOOK at the
sum total of your day. You've done nothing, and
consequently you are nothing.

You are doing fine.
Everything you have ever done was
attained by you, and everybody who loves
you does so because you are you. They love you for
who you are, regardless of your faults. They are here
for a reason. They really do love you. And sure, you might
have said something that you consider makes you look silly,
but there's no way he is thinking on the same level about it
as you. And sure, maybe the food was overcooked, but it
doesn't matter because it's only lunch. Wow. And look,
just LOOK at the sum total of your day. You might feel
like you've done nothing, but look, the reality is
that you achieved plenty, and anyway, it
doesn't matter, because there is
always tomorrow.

A trick of the trade I learned one day was the visual practice of 'labelling' my thoughts, so that every time a bad one came up, I envisioned stamping it with the label 'Bad Thought' and then discarding it to the back of my head like the Arc of the Covenant from Indiana Jones. Lost in a warehouse full of boxed up items never to be investigated again, except in an academic sense. From a severe distance. It was a neat little trick, because after all, bad thoughts aren't reality, they are just that. Bad Thoughts.

Does that mean that Good Thoughts are meaningless too? Well, if they derive from logical thinking, then absolutely not. It's just about knowing when to accept the thought, and when not to.

This brings us nicely to the most vital part of overcoming emotional distress. Loving yourself.

Loving You And Your Demons

Cognitive dissonance brought on by a negative inner voice is precisely why it is absolutely vital that we focus inwards, on our internal workings, and learn to love them, and by extent, to love ourselves.

Doing so is a complex process, especially if you've spent minimal time in life looking inwards, but engaging in it to a full extent so that you know yourself, understand yourself, and treat yourself well, in order that you can improve your internal being, first and foremost, will allow you, by extent, to be better to those around you.

Figure out you, and you've got the rest. It's as simple and as complicated as that.

Not convinced? Do you still feel that altruism is in fact the way to go? That helping others first is more important than helping oneself? Make others happy, and happiness is yours?

I will ask one question in response to this. At whose behest are you doing this? Is it for yourself, or to satisfy others? Perhaps it is both, but I will argue that helping others is a hopeless pursuit without first helping yourself.

I will analyse this in the spirit of Ayn Rand, who was against altruism as a principle. The idea that people have no right to exist for their own sake, and that service to others is the only justification for their existence, and that self sacrifice is their highest moral duty, is an ultimately dishonest path.

Now, I will not go so far as to uphold Rand's analysis of altruism, because I do not believe that altruism is the root of all evil in the world. In fact, I believe that it can be good for us, as well as others, because ultimately, if something we do makes us feel good on our own terms, be it the simple act of giving a homeless person some spare change or sacrificing your seat on the bus *to* someone in greater need, then it can't *be* an act of altruism, as it is ultimately serving *us*, even if it is also serving somebody else.

Nor will I say that Rand is somebody who should be put on a pedestal for her views, because they are very divisive. In fact, it can be argued that more people passionately disagree with her arguments than would claim, "Hey, she's got a point". A lot of that could be due to said detractors misinterpreting her viewpoint as being one that upholds a purely self serving nature, but the argument I will stand strong with, is this one here: This fundamental disagreement with the Self as the independent mind, that recognises no authority higher than its own, is deemed by society as an immoral stance, and given the projection of many societies around the globe being one of selflessness, and putting others first, something that nameless religions profess in their doctrines, it is no wonder that this disagreement exists.

I feel that a great many people have trouble kicking this belief out of their heads, so ingrained into their consciousness is the importance of putting others first. But it is important, mandatory even, that during times of emotional distress or faltering mental health, that we dismantle this doctrine.

I will once again stress that *You* are the most important entity in your life. That the things around you, be they people you hold, or the books on your shelf, or the games on your Xbox hard drive, are no good without your happiness. And so, reader, look at yourself. Inspect all of your traits, the things you both love and hate about yourself, and hug them, and I will talk about this very practice later on in this essay.

So, a great literary genius such as Ayn Rand may well have iconically declared altruism as the path to ruin, and referenced James Joyce as an altruistic figure, who married out of altruism, wanting to make a girl who was much worse off than him happy, resulting in this girl becoming increasingly unhappy over the years and eventually committing suicide (Yikes), but others equally profess the importance of the self, and of *you.*

Of course, I'm not here to make broad statements about altruism, or to claim that every altruistic deed results in a terrible end, as the last thing that this book intends to do is to tell you what philosophy to believe in. This recognition of Rand's stance is only to support my own claim that helping others at the expense of yourself can not make you happy. You must come first. Because you are important. If an iconic literary figure such as Rand is too intense a reference, let's look at today, because, weird as it may seem, this same philosophy is professed by modern media, in reality television, no less.

Ru Paul expresses this when he says, "If you can't love yourself, how in hell you gonna love anybody else?"

A modern example, for sure, and one that is resonating in the waves of an influential reality TV show that endorses inclusivity to such a degree as that particular show does, but hell, perhaps if James Joyce had seen it, he might've put himself first. Okay, probably not, but there we go.

Let's start by laying out all of the personal traits you consider to be negative, or at least, the ones that you are currently acutely aware of, that your inner voice is telling you are negative traits.

Sometimes we can do this to ourselves. We are intensely harsh, thinking things like: *Why am I so sensitive*, or *if only I wasn't so lazy*, et cetera, et cetera, it can go on and on, and we can find a hundred traits, and find seven flavours of negative as to why they are destructive or bad for us in some way or another.

But the truth is, that many human traits can be considered to be negative, if they are perceived to be that way. Have you ever heard somebody shoot somebody down for being opinionated, or blunt, or aggressive, or lazy, or emotional, or arrogant, or narcissistic, or or or or or...it goes on and on. Many, many traits can be perceived negatively.

To begin with a relatively tame example, when I was a boy, I was a fussy eater. I flat out refused to eat anything that I didn't 'like' (I had never even tried any of the foods I declared not to like) and I was told sternly by the almighty judges that were my parents, my dinner ladies, and even friends, that I was stubborn.

Stubborn, they spat at me, as though this was a bad thing.

Stubbornness can be perceived as a negative trait, and if it is perceived as negative, it is, sadly, and regrettably, internalised as negative.

But, much to the frustration of my parents, and indeed to the frustration of anybody who tried to force feed me peas, carrots or potatoes, I was proud of this label. *Stubborn,* I thought. *That's me. I own that. That's mine.* And own it I did. To this very day, I am still stubborn, and still proud of it. Because there are many positive results that stubbornness can achieve. How about resilience? During that aforementioned rough day at work, where your partner dumps you, and you refuse to cave in? Or running up to that important exam, not to let the tiredness break you? After all, stubbornness, by its very semantics, suggests sturdiness, forthrightness, and an unmoving nature.

Stubbornness is a strength, not a weakness.

Unfortunately, this was a rare occasion, that I was able to identify the characteristic that I was accused of being, as a golden crown. If only we could do this with every single one of the things we are programmed to think badly of, then we would be unstoppable, wouldn't we? I believe so.

Realistically, you can move through any number of personality traits that can be denoted as negative, and find a myriad of positive benefits. How about *impatience?*

God you are so impatient! They chide.

So what? Impatience yields many positive results. An impatient person isn't willing to wait around. They want things done *now.* They will work hard, try hard, and you know what, sometimes lack of patience achieves *results.* The same can be said for someone who is chided for being short tempered. Anger can be used as energy. No, you shouldn't smash your computer up when things get tough (but hey, if it helps, it *is* your property after all. I am a firm believer that breaking things for therapeutic reasons can be good, as long as it belongs to you, but acting out in anger can have harmful impacts, such as you not being able to use your computer anymore, due to it being a broken mess on the floor), nor should you punch your coworkers in the face (an action which *can* convincingly be argued as categorically helpful on a visceral level, but definitely don't do that) but anger can be used in other ways. Do you exercise? Whether it's cardio or lifting, it absolutely helps.

More on this later.

Are you creative? As a creative energy, anger can be a goldmine, no? For sure, there are situations where anger is unwanted, and absolutely unhelpful, but life is tough sometimes, and if you are someone who is prone to anger, let's face it, at some point you're gonna get angry. The trick is using it at the right time, for a productive purpose, and of course, not affecting anybody else.

Do I even need to explore the perceived negativity of overthinking and perfectionism? So many of us hard working people are cursed with this. It's no surprise that this can cause stress. When those deadlines are coming, and we just *have* to make sure that everything is perfect, that we've done the absolute best that we possibly can - that can result in us tearing our hair out. But look, is this really a bad thing? Tearing your hair out is, for sure, but the end result of your work bears so much fruit, and you might just create something that you're truly proud of. The trick with this one is to learn to reel it in at the right time. At one point are you just crossing and dotting the same I's and T's that have already been crossed? And at one point is your overthinking nothing more than dwelling on things which are not worth dwelling on?

Now, obviously there are thousands of traits that you might have, dear reader, including the ones listed before, and obviously I can't spell every single one of them and the solution out because then this book would be a thousand pages long and very boring indeed, but the top and tail of it is this: try and figure out what your particular set of traits are, and try and find the positive in them. That way, next time you are overwhelmed by it, or a negative perception of it, you will have provided yourself with a nuanced way of looking at it, which should hopefully become less overwhelming, over a period of time.

You can even consider things such as narcissism, arrogance or laziness, and it might seem as though I have cherry picked traits that are easier to defend, but I believe that positives can be found in every trait. Laziness is often a sign of intellect, for instance. George Orwell once said that all writers are lazy by nature, and others I could name make the claim that an intellectual person is likely to pursue intellectual things, while not bothering to tidy their rooms (I say this, unironically, without reference to Jordan Peterson, who I wasn't thinking of when I wrote that sentence, but categorically am now). Arrogance is often just a negative perception of self confidence, which is absolutely a positive thing. Take social situations. This is somewhere you might thrive due to self confidence. And narcissism, well, it is societally thought of as negative, but it carries with it so many wonderful things, such as positive self perception, which can help you a lot in life.

So try this. Write down the traits that are causing you to beat yourself up internally. The ones creating all that no good cognitive dissonance. Make a list, preferably, and then, opposite this list, list all of the positive traits you can think of. Remember all of the times that it helped you out in life. I will use stubbornness as my jumping off point, and hell, for variety, I'll even jot down the negatives.

Negative Traits	Positive Traits
Resistance to new things.	• Resilience.
	• Defiance to failure.
	• Defiance to odds.
	• Determination.
	• Strength.

Well, look at that. I gave myself five minutes and could only think of one negative trait. Perhaps my inner voice is particularly positive today, who knows, or perhaps there are less negatives to stubbornness than I thought. And so, I can conclude in this case that *other people*, and indeed *society as a whole*, could be the culprits of your negative internalisation, which is yet another reason why you must focus solely on *yourself* when dealing with these issues.

Because the harsh truth of the matter is that you will *never escape your traits.* I mean, maybe you can mitigate them, and squash them to a certain level, but they are never going to go away completely, and so what is the point, I ask you humbly and sincerely, *to name one singular useful purpose of* scalding yourself about them over and over and over again? If you can name one reason that is useful and productive, I will eat my computer. I'll wait.

scalding yourself is objectively bad for you. All it does is prolong the anguish of a particular voice. I have a friend who got into a relationship a few years back. Within two months of dating, they were pregnant. Oh, dear. Now, many would panic in this situation (I certainly would), but my friend did not. When, six months in, I asked him how he could stay so calm in a situation as life altering as this, he told me that stress would not prepare him for the situation. Because getting needlessly anxious about every little thing served no purpose other than to add more grief, for no gain. Because panicking does nothing for the situation. When the baby arrives, what use was all that stress? All it did was stress you out. A pointless exercise.

But sure, there are some things that are more challenging. There are some emotions that interrupt our lives much more than stubbornness or lack of patience. Some things are a little bit blacker than the aforementioned traits and need more work, but what I am getting at in a roundabout way here is that there is truly no escape from ourselves. The only thing we can do is *embrace ourselves*. That is the way to turn ourselves around. That is the key.

Embracing Yourself

Let's discuss the prospect of embracing oneself in more detail.

This is a nasty one, because it's where things begin to seem egotistical.

But that is exactly what you must do sometimes, in order to keep your head above water. Because the waves do duck you under in stressful times. Take today. As I type (or, as you read, whichever is appropriate) I am massively behind with work. I had social events planned which I then cancelled due to stress - I find social events particularly unpleasant at times, especially those where every single person invited to said event is somebody close to myself, thus marking me as the go to guy, or the leader. I - pardon my french - fucking despise being the leader of a group, it's just not in my nature. I am an introvert by nature, prone to being more of a second in command type, and acting as a leader gets exhausting fast, and that's if I even *have* the energy to begin with, and I rarely do.

As a result of cancelling this event, I felt immediately down. I took to my bed, and lay there for about thirty minutes, satisfying that limbic system by feeding emotions, almost to an indulgence. I thought about how frustrating the situation was, and generally dwelt on my misfortune. To make things worse, one of my friends was in the process of travelling a distance to see me, and so the burden of having to cancel the event was a great one. To this minute, he still hasn't responded to my message, and I felt so guilty about the prospect of diverting his route that I caved and sent a follow up message telling him to come anyway. Thus, I alleviated my guilt at having cancelled the evening at such short notice.

This is some negative stuff, let me tell you, and from the outside, it seems so simple. When I read it back, I expect I'll wonder just how I could allow myself to get into such a pit of cognitive dissonance and despair over something like this. Much of it was self imposed, to be sure, and all of it surely resolved with the simple imposition of some greater time management skills, but negative nonetheless, was my mindset.

Fortunately, I understand myself a heck of a lot better now than I did ten years ago, and so managing the situation was simpler, and a much more practical process.

Because as I lay there, grinding my teeth, staring grumpily at the ceiling, I noticed something. Over time, the limbic voice started to recede, while the prefrontal cortex voice got louder. I began to plan my newly shaped day. The result, after a period of time, was, I took to my desk and began to work, and within thirteen minutes wrote nearly a third of my quota. What did I write about? Why, you just read it. I wrote about my experience with the day. I spun my negative experience into a piece of work. I *embraced myself.*

Negative feelings, negative habits, however you wish to characterise them, have a profound impact on our day, and affect how we perceive the sum total of our day. A task that may have been a delight can become a drag, while a menial task can become a delightful break from the main task.

Now, let's take this further.

What would you say if I told you that I knew of a bonafide, psychologically proven method to help with your negative inner voice at any given moment?

Nonsense, you must be saying. **What, you think you have all the answers?**

Well, no. Not all the answers. But bear with me, because this is one of the most important pieces of practical advice I was ever given.

Grab a pen and paper, or open a word document, or the 'notes' app on your phone (mediums are endless nowadays!). Now, make a list of your ten greatest achievements, that were achieved on *your own terms*, at any point in your life. For the express purposes of this practice, you may only need five or six, but to be safe, list ten.

Now, write in detail each accomplishment, what it meant to you, and why it was such a darn good achievement. Write in some depth, a paragraph perhaps, or hell, if you feel like it, keep on going as long as you can.

By the time you've listed three achievements in detail you will already feel better about yourself.

But for God's sake, don't stop there!

Keep at it until you have ten solid accomplishments listed. And there, you have it. The ultimate spirit lifter in a crisis. Make sure you have this list close to hand, preferably on a sheet of laminated paper, hanging on your office wall, or in a drawer, so that you can grab it and read it at any given time.

It is psychologically proven that this method helps. Picture it. You have a bad day in some form, in a way that affects your self esteem. A work failure, maybe even a relationship falter of some kind, or anything in between that makes you feel bad. Just grab hold of that list, and read through it slowly. I'm willing to bet that you won't even *need* to read the entire ten accomplishments before you start to lift again. Three or four is bound to do the trick. Five, to be safe.

Furthermore, perhaps at some point you will get worn out reading the same achievements over and over again. You've read it a thousand times already and the impact is starting to fade, or perhaps the things you listed don't apply to the particular emotion felt at the present moment. Not a problem. Just rearrange the list so that number ten is number one, or however you wish to keep it fresh. Perhaps different forms of failure require different achievements to lift you. So be it, this is your list and it should be designed to work singularly for you. Think of some things that counteract your negative emotions.

To reiterate the point introduced in the first essay, *You are important,* and by extension so are your achievements. Maintaining yourself, and not falling into that black hole, is a part of this. Treat yourself well, indulge in your achievements, and let them override those emotions. *Embrace* yourself. *Hug* yourself. *Love* yourself.

Practicing The Pavlovian You

When I was younger, I had trouble waking up. I'll be honest, I still do. But the thing is, back then it was a *problem*, because I kept on beating myself up about it. Scalding my nature. Rippling into my worthless self for being so damn incompetent. Why can't you just be *normal?* I'd ask myself, and go on tearing my hair out over and over again, morning after morning. Or rather, afternoon after afternoon.

During this frustrating period of time, I tried a number of things attempting to rectify this 'problem'. Firstly, by scattering alarms around my room.

Didn't work.

Why?

Well, because even my exhausted brain knew where to find the alarms. As if I had subconsciously noted their locations during my sleep, I got so fast at switching them off that I was back in bed before my bedsheets, which I had thrown off at the moment the first alarm erupted, landed. Fail.

I even bought one of those noisey, cacophonous alarms on wheels that rolls off of your bedside desk and screams until you are forced to get up and find it. Thirty pounds down the drain. Within a week I had smashed it to pieces.

Did I ever find a solution? Yes, yes I did. And I would have gotten away with it too if it weren't for you meddling kids. If you'll permit me to sound quite insane for a paragraph or two, I can explain why this new method was effective, and how I believe that the path to mitigating emotional strife can be, to a degree, a simple case of ringing a metaphorical pavlovian bell.

The solution to waking up at a certain, decent time was not a case of making noise so unbearable I simply had to shut it off, nor was it a situation of putting another irritating obstacle in my path, that I would inevitably get angry at and destroy, but a matter of practicing the process of waking up. What I did, and how I figured this out remains a mystery to me, was clean my teeth, wash my face, and go lie in the dark, having set an alarm. I was wide awake. Bear in mind I was doing this in the middle of the day.

I lay there, eyes closed, as if lying in, and then, suddenly...

BEEP BEEP BEEP BEEP BEEP!

went the alarm, and I shot up, got out of bed, and got going. I practiced this again and again and again and again, going through the rigmarole of the bedtime routine, only to leap up when my alarm went off. Lying in the dark, and then leaping up. Once I had repeated this process enough times, I went about my day. Bed time arrived, actual bed time, probably around 5AM, with my alarm set for a reasonable time. I slept like normal.

When the alarm went off, I leapt up.

The practice of shooting out of bed the instant that *BEEP BEEP BEEP BEEP* began had worked its way into my subconscious brain. My brain and body now leapt up when that sound blared out, in the same way that Pavlov's dogs might have when they heard that bell. Now, where's the damn food at?

Sad to say I didn't keep this up for very long, but during my commitment to it, it worked. Is there any reason why we can't use similar tactics when dealing with emotional issues?

It is impossible not to dwell sometimes. We have to. Things happen that challenge us, or confront us. Sometimes a customer will accost us about the price of a meal, the lack of a strawberry in their pink gin; a result of their being no strawberries left that *you*, the incompetent bartender, did not advise them of. Things like this can be frustrating.

Perhaps it's a more extreme case. An unpleasant memory disturbs you. We all have negative encounters, bad memories, some more severe than others, but that fact does not serve to mitigate the unpleasantness of each and every person's negative emotions pertaining to these encounters and memories. But is there not a way that we can snap away from these feelings, so that they don't disturb us to our core, but only hurt us to a certain point? Similar to the technique with the laminated achievements list, try this one out.

When something disturbs you in this nature, don't try to fight the strife, because on some level your brain might just need to reflect on it. Thinking about things is *not inherently negative*, because doing so is often just the processing of information, which is something your brain will do from time to time in order to *help* you get through things. So, sit down, set an alarm and reflect. Don't fight it. The denial of such things can actually be more harmful to you in the long term. Think it through, allow your brain to do its thing...

BEEP BEEP BEEP BEEP BEEP!

Now stop. Get up, and go. You thought about the issue to an appropriate degree, and now end. Get on with your day. If you find you need to dwell again, do it. But don't allow the process to go on for longer than is appropriate for solving the issue.

Are there any other scenarios that we can apply this method to? Ones where it is a little more tricky to overcome?

How about when that intrusive memory leaps at you, or when your partner dumps you and you're lying in bed staring at the ceiling, or when anxiety overrides you? Can this practice be used effectively in these circumstances?

Granted, it might not be the easiest thing to do, but as with a lot of things, it is a *practice*, just like the laminated list, just like simple breathing exercises, or meditation, or exercising, painting, fishing - the simplicity of it can be complex, in that you, reader, have to find your own loves, distractions and focuses in order to direct your energy to the correct places at the appropriate times, but if you can pinpoint them, figure out what your triggers are, and know yourself better than ever, these practices should get easier and easier to integrate.

Productive Paralysis

Now, onto something we all have emotional issues with. Productivity.

Waking up is no longer an issue, because I stopped scalding myself about it. There are a host of things we can stop being so hard on ourselves about, and the crowned jewel of these is productive paralysis.

What is productive paralysis?

I may have taken some liberty with my phrasing of the condition, but it is an accurate way of describing a certain catatonic state that many of us who aspire to better things experience.

Ever found yourself lying around longer than you should, only to then motivate yourself, grab some coffee and then sit down to apply for those jobs, or start that project...only to find yourself watching TV, playing video games, or fiddling with two pennies and a paperclip for hours on end, only to then realise that *whoops,* the sun is going down and you've wasted your entire evening and it's time to go to bed soon? Oh well, what a write off. But it's okay, there's tomorrow, right?

Guess what happens the next day?

That's right. The same damn thing.

This could go on for weeks. Months. The longest it went on for me was about a year and a half. I'd be waiting for that precious weekend, so that I could start doing the things that really mattered to me, the things that would take my life forward...only to find myself doing nothing when the moment of freedom finally arrived. For such a long time I thought I was lazy. Family members and friends would even accuse me of laziness. And, the gullible person that I was, I believed them, and continued to beat myself up day after day, week after week, about my hopeless, lazy nature. *When did this happen? I used to have so much drive. Where did it all go?*

Some reading and gathering information taught me that, well, it didn't go *any*where. It was there the whole time, it was just trapped between a rock and a hard place.

If you have found yourself in this situation, consider that you are not *lazy*, but *paralysed*.

When we want to do something, but are afraid of doing it, due to the potential of it failing, we can find ourselves in a catatonic state. The drive isn't gone, nor the motivation, the creativity, the impetus, the beating pulse of the drive - it's just that the fear of failure stops us from going ahead, resulting in us existing in this state.

For creative types, inventive types and entrepreneurial types, failing at something they care about, even if it's a subjective failure, sends them further back than when they began. It knocks them into the abyss, because it matters so much to them. The potential black hole of this is a big, deep, scary one, a daunting one, and so people slip into a kind of paralysis. It takes incredible bravery and an intense tolerance to break through this wall. To be honest, I can't blame you for being catatonic. It is completely understandable. This is *hard*.

For dealing with this, I will lay out a two pronged strategy.

First, make your brain believe that it is okay. It is not a sign of hopelessness, nor is it a shadow of your spineless, bone idle nature. If anything, it is a sign of great things to come. It means there is a lot going on inside of you, and at some point it is gonna show in all its beautiful colour, and so realise that it is there, respect that it needs time, and don't beat yourself up. Nurture it. Love it. It's another vital part of you and it should be held close...but if productivity is not ready to happen, forcing it could be futile. Rather, the strategy here is to accept things for what they are.

That is prong one, and we will explore it a little more in a paragraph or two.

Prong two is this: set reasonable targets.

But to complicate it, here is a slightly more convoluted phrasing of said prong. Set unreasonable targets.

When I say unreasonable, I mean that if your project is too daunting at present, set yourself a miniscule target that any person, no matter how busy they are, could make. Five minutes, ten, three. Something that is unnoticeable, but counts towards the ultimate goal.

I do believe it is important to set yourself a short, manageable timeframe within which to set out to take a step towards your goals. Again, set a timer to something small and manageable, even with the obstacle of a full time job. How about thirty minutes? We can all fit thirty minutes into our day, right? If even that is too much, try twenty minutes, fifteen, even ten. The key isn't to spend endless hours every day devoted to The Thing, but to take regular stabs at it. Ten minutes, every single working day? Why, if you stick to this, by Friday you'll have spent fifty minutes on it, which might not seem like much, but it's obviously better than nothing, and a week is a short amount of time. Another week and you'll have spent an hour and forty minutes on The Thing. A month and...

You get the picture.

The fact is, that while it might not feel like much, or anything at all, when you look at the sum total of your efforts after a period of time, you might just surprise yourself at the results. And, if you are expecting not to be happy with the result, and this is holding you back from doing that ten minute stretch, I'm willing to bet that the space between work efforts will provide you with the distance needed from your project for you to remain objective when looking back over it.

And again, I will stress this point. If approaching The Thing is still too hard, and you need to go back to catatonia for a little while longer, *it is okay*. Go right back to it. Just work and chill out, socialise, whatever you do, and feel that pressure immediately lift. Because the reality is that sometimes, when we want to do something and it doesn't happen, it isn't for want of anything lacking. It might just be that it isn't the right time. How many famous entrepreneurs can you find, who didn't get their big break until they were in their fifties or sixties? Later, in some cases. Charles Bukowski didn't get famous until he was fifty. H.P Lovecraft didn't see one ounce of recognition for his life's work until *after he was dead*. There are a million other people I could mention.

So that, in a nutshell, is what it is all about.

Prong one, it is okay. Embrace it, crave it, and love and nurture another aspect of yourself.

Prong two, set small, achievable targets that you can stab at regularly.

The momentum you can build may just result in dismantling the catatonia. Reminder, that catatonia is not the enemy. It is not a fire breathing beast that we have to annihilate to survive. It is a part of you, and fighting it only creates further cognitive dissonance for the inner voice. The first time I wrote the first sentence of this paragraph out, I wrote *The momentum you can build may just result in breaking that wall of catatonia down.* I changed it, because I did not want to portray this strategy as some kind of attack on the state, because treating aspects of your character as demons to be fought does nothing for our self esteem. It only serves to deny self acceptance, when the trick of incorporating all of these methods and thought processes into your daily life is one of lifting the inner turmoil off of your chest so that you can focus on what's in front of you, and accept yourself, and the situation.

Now, since we are talking about productivity, it seems appropriate, and even mandatory to address the dragon in the room. Procrastination.

Ah yes, procrastination, our perceived worst enemy. Haunting our dreams, and our days, standing in the way. Your time has come.

It may surprise you, reader, to learn that our method of dealing with this little piggy is not to hate it, but to embrace it.

Before you roll your eyes, hear us out, because this links straight back to a previous essay.

Procrastination occurs when the limbic system and the prefrontal cortex are fighting one another for your attention, your focus. It grows stronger when we entertain it. For instance, the desire for a chocolate biscuit becomes much more tangible when one is faced with a packet of said biscuits. The impulse to check our phones becomes huge when we hear them go *ting!* and so on. The limbic system, being deeper embedded and ultimately more powerful than the prefrontal cortex, often wins, but this has been discussed already.

Procrastination is one more thing that we simply need to accept and embrace. Despite it being something we can control, or even shut out to a degree, there is an argument to be made that it carries positive results.

For instance, today I suffered from a case of writer's block. Now, a few years ago I suffered with the same issues discussed within these pages. Catatonia. Paralysis. The inability to write anything substantial at all due to the abject fear that the result of my efforts would reflect my ineptitude to such a level that I would die inside. As a result I spent more time drinking and, pardon my french, pissing around, than being productive. At the time I viewed it in such a negative light that it added to the negativity in my inner voice. The answer that I craved and eventually found was that I needed to stop trying as hard. That it wasn't the right time. That forcing results was not the thing to do, because the results I ended up with were forced. Had I been more patient, and realised that the flow would come back, as well as the impetus and the drive, as well as the creative magic, I might've realised that when the time finally arrived, the results would have been better.

Today was the same. Yes, I might not have started working until later than I would have liked, but when I began, results came faster, more fully formed than they might have otherwise.

Procrastination is a part of the process. And if you stop beating yourself up about it, perhaps you can enjoy it rather than letting it eat you alive.

One of the writers of *The Sopranos* talked about this once. About the process of writing an entire screenplay in two weeks, and how he knew from the get go that he wasn't going to do any work for the first three or four days, and instead devoted those hours to working out, seeing movies or whatnot, rather than staring blankly in front of the computer, torturing himself; and it's a good strategy, in honesty. If you know you're going to be stagnant, or blocked, why torture yourself? Ask yourself, for real, why? If you can come up with an answer that justifies the deprecation, then you've found it.

So do something else for a while. Feel that passion build and build and trust that the spark will appear.

Starting From Zero

This is potentially a more subjective method, but it fits right in. Each day, start from zero.

That's right. Sun comes up. Pull up your blinds, grab your coffee, and nothing matters. You've got zero so far today, because it's a new day.

Does it sound negative, working your brain to see every day as one that begins at absolute zero? Perhaps it sounds that way, but think it through.

Every day brings challenges, right? Each task, shift, or appointment adds to our input of the day. Absolutely. Some days, we are just responding to the external stuff. When the time comes for us to focus on ourselves, we might be too exhausted from the external things to really give it a go, because we are held back by the events of before.

Well, if you can figure out how to mitigate, or at least minimise whatever it is that's poisoning your inner voice, whether it's by using the information laid out in these essays, or simply using the essays as a jumping off point to figuring it out yourself, and you're at this point having done this, then perhaps you're feeling more positive already and are able to limit any damage done to your inner voice throughout the trials and tribulations of everyday life.

But make no mistake, everyday life can be hard. Sometimes, the mere act of getting up, making a coffee and going to your desk to do an hour's work can feel like pulling teeth without anaesthetic, let alone dealing with full time jobs when times are busy, maintaining a relationship that's travelling through a trough stage rather than a peak stage, or a kid, or two kids, or hell, all of the above, for many people.

Now, again, this book is all about you. Focusing on yourself, and allowing your inner strength and happiness to be your focal point, so that any and all of the other factors will be better off as a result of your new found strength, determination, drive, whatever it is you are seeking, and one more way that we can heal ourselves is by starting fresh each and every day.

That is what starting from zero each day is. But how can we achieve this feeling? How can we bury yesterday, and soldier on as if nothing happened?

Well, as always, burying things is not the solution. Burying and suppressing things only pushes them into a corner, and as we've said before, processing information to its appropriate degree (a clinical way of saying, dwell on things, but a more positive one. We, as thinking machines, have to process information we receive) can be helpful, as long as we practice the act of stealing ourselves before we go from processing to overthinking, overfeeling, and all those kinds of things which simply lead to unnecessary dissonance. But there are many

73

things we can do to start from zero each day. I will share some, and give my own perspective.

My life requires me to work on multiple large writing projects, and it is easy for me to slip into the habit of looking at one day as a simple continuation of the one before, and things gradually begin to not feel like achievements at all. Indeed, when you're staring at a word processor and typing most of the day, and then the next day returning to the word processor and continuing from where you left off, it is understandable why this might happen. However, with the simple act of accounting for my progress at the end of each day, i.e logging my word count, filing the effort away with a timestamp, I am able to look at the outcome with a deal more satisfaction and separation.

There are many things you can do to achieve this same result. Try timing your tasks, setting a forty five minute timer for each task.

Understandably, that is unlike a situation when you are working a full time job, for instance. A separation between work life and home life is important too.

This has largely been a discussion of productivity. But, how does this fit into the emotional stuff?

Again, there are actions we can take to refresh ourselves. Are negative things affecting you? Do you have any mouldering resentments or things that bothered or upset you? Here's another psychologically advised technique that works for some people. Take a piece of paper (or a few pieces of paper, depending on how many things are on your mind) and write the thing down. Take the paper, fold it up, and put it in a box, and put the box away. I believe the idea of putting the issues in a box is that you can open the box at a later time, and reflect on the things that bothered you that day. Big or small, put it in the box. Make sure it's the kind of box you can fasten and close properly. The psychological trick here is obvious, that you've transferred the issue from your head onto a piece of paper, and put it away. It's not gone, it's away for safekeeping. But most importantly, It's out of your head.

Negativity	Imposter Syndrome	Guilty
Anger	Intrusive thoughts	Strife

Perhaps you'd prefer to burn the paper, and I can't fault you for that. There is great satisfaction that comes with burning the issues, watching them catch fire and turn to blackened ash in a matter of seconds. Wonderful. But bear in mind, once they're gone, they're gone. Also bear in mind the possibility that it is more cleansing to burn them. That's the route I would take. Personally, I hate the idea of there being a box full of issues I've had just sitting under my bed for me to remember, but that's just me. This is about you.

Now, look around the house. Are there other things we can do? Sure there are.

Have you tried rearranging your bedroom? Refreshing the sheets? Cooking something completely new from scratch? Taking a route to work that you wouldn't usually take? Visiting shops you walk by without a care in the world, to buy your lunch from there instead of your usual place? Are there different ways you can work? Different stationary folders you can buy to store your paperwork? Green instead of black?

These are all minor, *minor* things, but you might be surprised at the subtle psychological effect they have on you in terms of refreshing your day. Remember, starting from zero is an excellent way to validate your accomplishments, rid yourself of lingering emotional filament, and start again, not having forgotten what happened yesterday, but having moved on from it.

Moving Through the Motions

Somebody once told me that momentum creates momentum, and meant it literally. As in, do some running, and you'll be better.

That is, for sure, not what you want to hear when you're in a dark place. They are the kind of words that make you bristle and bear your teeth, resulting in the assailant backing the hell off. Hopefully. If they know what's good for them. I mean, how dare they imply that it's that simple, and it isn't.

When dealing with issues like depression, it is very hard to accept anybody telling you that the answer is simple to put some white shoes on and run. Running isn't exactly some kind of intellectual pursuit. It is simply putting one foot in front of the other over and over and over and over and over and over and over again.

But loathe as I am to admit it, determined as one might be to gnash their teeth at anybody bold enough to confront them with a solution as simple and brainless as putting one foot in front of the other rapidly over and over again, their foot cushioned by some daft white shoe with striped colours on it, that looks like a high tech toothbrush, they are frustratingly right.

To a degree.

Of course, there are things that exercise can't necessarily fix, but I will admit that it can unequivocally alleviate things like anxiety. If you were to measure any negative emotion before and after a hefty cardio workout, or an intense lifting session, there is an argument to be made that these things are lessened *after* the exercise, due to physical exhaustion.

Take the COVID-19 lockdown situation as a prime example. During this time it was easy to fall into a sedentary habit, and I am completely guilty of it. The start of the lockdown was different in this respect to later on, because there was a greater determination to maintain structure, to jog and keep momentum up. Culture shock had a lot to do with this. Culture shock and fear. Why fear? Why, because fear of going insane kept us moving. But as time went on, we became used to the lack of structure, to living a sedentary lifestyle, until eventually our step counters died of neglect. Not that step counters are an accurate depiction of *anybody's* exercise habits. How often is your phone sitting on a table charging? Or not in your hands? We can't trust our step counters. Throw them in the bin.

Now, further to my initial (and I suppose, as I'll explore shortly, ignorant) perception of exercise as a non-intellectual pursuit, it was at this point that intellectual pursuits began. Perhaps it's the same for many people, that when we stop moving, we are put into a situation where we are required to find new outlets to spend our energy on. Jigsaws, vlogs, reading, watching films and over analyzing them to the point where we wonder what on earth we are doing with our lives anymore, what have you, but it's granted that new habits develop in situations such as these, meanwhile the simple, therapeutic act of putting one foot in front of the other, a thing that is proven to improve energy levels and mood, is on the (no pun intended here, which of course, as an astute reader, you will realise means, pun massively intended) backfoot.

And then we complain that we don't have energy.

It is only once we begin to move around again that we realise the momentum that is created by our momentum.

I won't go on and on about the chemical benefits of exercise. The release of endorphins and all that, because it's an obvious fact that psychologists, vloggers and basically every person on the planet at this point, professe. Yes, that's well documented. Rather, I will focus on the explorative, adventurous aspect of it, because I believe that is the most important benefit. Of seeing fields, different houses, riverboat communities, whatever is at your doorstep. Because exploring outside of the four walls I lived in was the trump card to my ignorance. Movement creates energy, and not only that, but it *can* be an intellectual pursuit. How many things can you think about when you're walking somewhere previously unexplored? How many philosophical journeys can you go on? How many creative ideas might bubble and stew in your mind while you do it? Or entrepreneurial ideas? Or hell, perhaps a simple breath of fresh air after a hard day?

During my run today, I was accosted by a dog, smiled at by several strangers, and even witnessed a second dog chase a kid off his skateboard. No, these dogs weren't black dogs, but stories to tell. Experiences to store in my head, rather than the same beige walls or video games, or computer screens.

I'm certainly glad to have had those encounters.

Managing Your Mental Health

Well, I've saved the best two for last. The whopper.

I'll admit that one scenario I felt unable to mention in the *Practicing the Pavlovian You* essay, is the descent of depression. Why? Well, because it is the only scenario that is impossible to avoid with this method. Depression, whether it is simply a chemical imbalance brought on by the journey of your travels through the motions of life, or a sudden and inexplicable black cloud out of nowhere, just isn't fun. Many of us who suffer with anxiety, especially those of us with a self-deprecating sense of humour, can find lots of comedic relief with it. The sheer absurdity of being too jittery and self conscious to go buy a sandwich or the terrible fear of a pub full of people, whom we have to weave awkwardly through to reach our one friend who is buried deep within the pub, has a lot of potential to make us laugh at ourselves. To find levity. And this kind of levity is never possible with depression. Depression is too damn horrible. Ask anybody who deals with it and they will tell you that the process is one of feeling like absolute shit, and then eventually getting through things. And that is why I have devoted an entire essay to it, because the hardest things in life are the most important to learn how to cope with.

This essay won't provide a direct solution, because, let's face it, nobody has found one and so to profess one would be ignorant, pretentious and completely inappropriate, but I hope it will be a helpful discussion.

Let's start with the black dog analogy. A poem we are all familiar with by this point, I am sure.

Whether or not we find it helpful is another thing entirely.

The poem describes its solution as one of controlling, managing and taking care of said black dog. Sure, we can do this. Or rather, we can *learn* to do this. But that takes some time. Depression has many different levels, that is to say, varying severities of dog bites, and the more severe ones can be overwhelming. When those fangs are dripping with your blood, and the glaring eye of the inexplicably wrathful dog is continuously watching you as you eat, sleep, and wash dishes, its force can be so great that it stops you from living your life.

So what about those times?

After all, a wound is a wound and some of those bites cut deep. When such a descent is imminent, how do you manage your black dog? You need a lot of strength, and anybody dealing with this kind of thing, and coping with it, is as strong as a bull, there is no doubt. But sometimes, just as described previously in other essays, the best thing is to nurse that wound, and I will go into that a little bit here.

Sometimes, the whole *get up and go* attitude is an unreasonable one, in fact it can be rage inducing at the wrong time. The idea that we can shake off these issues by forcing ourselves through them and *cracking on,* is just silly, and anybody preaching it needs a reality check.

I once had a friend. We worked together. One day a mutual friend of ours died. Won't get into it. It was very sudden and it devastated us. But it devastated my friend more than myself though, because the two of them were closer. The very next day, he went straight back to work and proceeded to have the worst number of shifts in his life. I'd find him face down on the desk, crying, and when I asked him what was wrong he told me this: "I really, really don't wanna be here."

The absurdity of the situation was this: in my opinion, he shouldn't have been there. What good did that do? Doing so, he had subjected himself to one of the most difficult days of his life. This seems like a harsh thing, that is, to claim that it was his fault in any way, and I am not saying that, but a situation like that is objectively self imposed. He didn't have to be there. He could have called in, and told his employers that he wasn't coming in, and granted himself the space he needed to deal with his issues.

The ones who profess that resilience is key and that the better way to go through something like this is to go to work so that you can focus on something other than your grief, are ignorant, in my view. If you are in a situation like this, or hell, if the black dog bites you out of nowhere, you owe it to yourself to help yourself. This goes back to a previous point about focusing on trauma, or negativity, to its appropriate level, in order that you can process that information.

Say, for instance, you get dumped, and it comes out of nowhere. It could happen to any of us, right? It is very much the same thing in this instance. How do you move on from a situation like this when you spend your days pushing the information into the corner of your head? To me, this seems like the path to prolonging pain, as some are determined to do.

Let's be clear. Sometimes it is true that - and I'm quoting an underground punk band from New York right now, the gems of wisdom come from all manner of places - a mindset is a choice you can make. You simply need to make the choice. To be better than the negative voices. To come up and say, okay, I'm going to do something good today, in spite of the worst voices. However, sometimes it is not possible, and the thing to remember here, as always, is this: *It's okay.*

That's right. It is okay to not be okay. It is okay not to be productive, or to cancel all of your social events. Staring at the ceiling, aloneness and meditation can be great practices in a situation such as this. Let's examine the thought processes that might come with shutting ourselves away for the day to process information in any way we choose, and look at the potential negatives that come with *it's not okay*, and then look at the antithesis.

It is not okay.	It is okay.

1) I haven't done any work today.	1) If I recharge, I can do more tomorrow.
2) I've cancelled my plans.	2) The next time I have plans, I will make the most of it.
3) I feel terrible and hopeless.	3) It won't last forever. Pain is temporary and when it goes, I might just feel better than ever.

The sheer ambiguity of the black dog poem can be frustrating at times, if we use it as a bonifided perspective on a mental condition. However, in its simplicity (and again, the ambiguity allows for this), it is reminding us that what it is about, fundamentally, is *damage control.*

When the dark clouds descend, the best we can do is limit the damage it causes. That is to say, employ the practices and skill sets learned so far, and minimise its impact on our lives as much as we can.

One practice here that will help could be the laminated list of accomplishments. If we think about those, we can begin to find ways to counteract our depression. If you can pinpoint your triggers, perhaps that will give you some clue as to what to include on your list. Truthfully, this has to be done when all is well, which is tough. Those of us that suffer intense mental health issues often feel that when our depression lifts, it can feel as if it never happened at all. Like a dream, almost. And just like dreams, all the information processed during that time gets dumped.

It's true, though, is it not? As a species we are self preserving. Our subconscious takes care of many issues for us, in its own way. For instance, there exists the fallacy that dreams are important, that they are trying to tell us something we aren't able to see in our day to day lives.

What is my stance on this issue? Well, quite bluntly, I believe it is nonsense.

Why?

Well, for one, if it were true that dreams carried vital information, we would remember them. Human beings have survival instincts. When a Thing is important, our brains retain it. They don't dump it like a hot plate. Regardless of whether you can remember your dreams intimately, and whether they contain some element of truth in them, I will argue that the element of truth that they carry is one of emotion. We have already spent quite some time expressing an aversion to some emotions, and how they can be irrational, invalid, and point towards something not really there, and that, indeed, satisfying said emotions only serves to enable the limbic system's insatiable appetite.

Further to this, I feel it can be the same with depression. The emotions conjured during such painful times as these can stem from irrational places, and indulging them creates immediate satisfaction on an emotional level, instead of logic and diplomacy prevailing. Swooping in to save us from the barrel of the abyss

Logic diminishes during depressive periods, it is true, and emotion takes hold, and our tendency to delve into negative emotions rises.

But what happens as the depression gradually begins to lift? It slowly, but surely, goes away, does it not?

Have you ever taken note of the thoughts you have during depression? Have any of them ever carried over?

Do these things haunt you on any other level other than the period of the depression?

If it is a persistent issue, write it down, and then find a counteraction to it. Use logic and diplomacy while it is present, so that you can bring it to your eyes during the dark periods, process it over and over again. Read it aloud, maybe. Your brain, the sponge that it is, will start to believe it if you say it over and over and over again. And so, give it some good news. Throw that dog a treat.

But never let your depressive voice seem reasonable, because it isn't. You are excellent, and are doing brilliantly, regardless of what your head tells you.

This is the ultimate damage control. A stiff lead for the black dog. One made out of logic, reason and reality. Now, pull that chain.

Becoming The Ultimate You

The infinite universe theory talks of infinite realities, and by extension, infinite possibilities. That means that theoretically, there are infinite Yous. Every variation of every You. Think about going to the kitchen and making a cup of tea. Across the infinite universes, are there infinite Yous, making infinite variants of infinite teas? Somewhere, out there, does the perfect cup of tea exist? The, if you'll once again pardon my horrible personality shining through, *infinitea?*

I believe that the answer to that question is *yes*, and so much more than that, reader, I believe that it is the one that *you* created.

What on Earth am I talking about? I'm talking about the ultimate You. I believe that the Ultimate You is, well, You, and if you can become that, you will win over all of the issues. But by doing so, like the tea, you may just create a different person. One who is more in control of themselves than ever before. One who knows themselves. Because the key to creating the ultimate you, the one in infinity, is to know yourself, and embrace yourself, and learn as much as you can about your traits, tendencies and inner workings. What does your inner voice say, and why does it say it? Examine it. If it's logistically wrong, teach yourself to recognise why. Counteract this. Act with reason, logic, and reality. Diplomacy, that is what it is. The more we can learn to reason the truth, the more we will limit damage to our emotions, and the happier we will be, the better off we will be. Freed from dissonance, to a progressive degree.

Create a strong structure of reason. Not a cast iron level of strength, but strong enough to prevail. Because we can't be perfect all of the time, nor can we be happy or triumphant twenty four seven, fifty two, but we can always aim to be our best selves, and the more we believe in this, the more we implement positivity and self love into our lives, the greater our creation will be.

Take the placebo effect. A body healing itself psychosomatically, merely by *believing* in the false cure presented to it. To some, the idea that this works is *magic*. But in reality it is not. Not on any level. Because theoretically, it can be explained scientifically, just like brain chemistry. Sure, we might not have the resources, intellect, or ability to explain it, but explain it we could, if we did have said resources.

So that is the thing with emotion, voice, and all of the concepts discussed in this book as a whole. They are all scientific things. We might not be able to explain them fully, but they *are* scientific. That means that there is logic to them, and therefore that logic can be applied *to* them. *There are answers.* Sometimes things seem complex, and to be sure, they are, internally, but some of the solutions, the baseline things, can be simple.

We think of thoughts and emotions as these ethereal things. These magical, untouchable pieces of fairy dust that are no different than, say, the dancing colours that appear in your retina when you close your eyes and stare at a bright light, but in reality, they are real. Physically real. Just as real as the ground you stand on, or the sky that you stare at. They are real, and they are all parts of you.

Life, after all, is not about finding yourself, as is professed by many, and mainly people who wear backpacks and play acoustic guitars, but about *creating yourself*, so get creating, and be the Ultimate You.

You.

Disclaimer

This book contains opinions and ideas of the author and is meant to teach the reader informative and helpful knowledge while due care should be taken by the user in the application of the information provided. The instructions and strategies are possibly not right for every reader and there is no guarantee that they work for everyone. Using this book and implementing the information/recipes therein contained is explicitly your own responsibility and risk. This work with all its contents, does not guarantee correctness, completion, quality or correctness of the provided information. Misinformation or misprints cannot be completely eliminated.

Printed in Great Britain
by Amazon

68047241R00066